The Compass

A Personal Guide for

Seeking, Finding, and

Following God's Direction

To Ronnie,
Wishing you many
happy journeys.

The Compass

A Personal Guide for

Seeking, Finding, and

Following God's Direction

GARY A. USERY

Pleasant Word
A Division of WINEPRESS PUBLISHING

Pleasant Word (a division of WinePress Publishing, PO Box 428, Enumclaw, WA 98022) functions only as book publisher. As such, the ultimate design, content, editorial accuracy, and views expressed or implied in this work are those of the author.

Acknowledgments: Thanks to Mom and Dad for the editing and encouragement.

Unless otherwise noted, all Scriptures are taken from the *Holy Bible, New International Version*. Copyright © 1973, 1978, 1984 by International Bible Society. Used by permission of Zondervan Publishing House.

Scripture verses marked LB are from *The Living Bible*, © 1971 by Tyndale House Publishers. Those marked CBW are from *New Testament: A Translation in Language of the People*, by Charles B. Williams, © 1965 by Edith S. Williams.

Excerpts from *Experiencing God*, by Henry Blackaby and Claude King, © 1994 by Broadman and Holman Publishers, used by permission.

Excerpts from *My Utmost for His Highest* by Oswald Chambers, edited by James Reimann, © 1992 by Oswald Chambers Publications Assn., Ltd. Original Edition © 1935 by Dodd Mead & Co., renewed 1963 by the Oswald Chambers Publications Assn., Ltd., and are used by permission of Discovery House Publishers, Box 3566, Grand Rapids, MI 49501. All rights reserved.

Excerpts from *Finding the Elusive Will of God*, copyright © 2005 by Michael Bronson, used by permission.

Excerpt from *Dynamics of Spiritual Gifts* by William J. McRae, copyright © 1976 by the Zondervan Corporation, used by permission of the Zondervan Corporation.

Lyrics from *Love Song* by Johnny Mac Powell, Mark Lee, Bradley B. Avery, Samuel Tai Anderson, and David Carr, © 1996 New Spring, Inc. All rights reserved, used by permission.

ISBN 1-4141-0754-4
Library of Congress Catalog Card Number: 2006905555

Table of Contents

Introduction

The fate of unborn millions will now depend, under God, on the courage and conduct of this army.

—Gen. George Washington

The fate of a nation hung in the balance. After a series of humiliating defeats, the battered and dispirited Continental Army of Gen. George Washington fled headlong in retreat. At best, Washington had about 3,000 troops, many of whom were in tatters. Making the situation more calamitous, the enlistments of two-thirds of these soldiers expired in less than two weeks. General Washington faced a crucial decision: continue the retreat and salvage what remained of his ragtag army or turn and attack.

General Washington decided to change direction and fight. In the midst of a howling winter storm, General Washington and his troops crossed the Delaware River and, in a battle that changed the fortunes of a war, of a nation, and of the world, defeated the Hessians at Trenton.

Few people face decisions of such consequence. However, you do face decisions that affect your life, the lives of those around you, and quite probably the lives of people whom you do not even know.

Decisions regarding family, relationships, finances, and career are all of great importance to you.

Several years ago my wife and I faced such a decision. Our three-year-old son was, at the time, the only grandchild on both sides of our family. We lived only a two-hour drive from both sets of grandparents, and my wife was eight months pregnant with our daughter. While I was out of the country on a business trip, my employer informed me that the office where I worked was being closed by new ownership. I had a choice to either relocate to another facility farther away from our families or take a severance package and look for a new job.

The infamous American philosopher Yogi Berra once advised, "When you come to a fork in the road, take it!"[1] A memorable quote, but it provides little help when faced with a difficult decision. How do you make important decisions similar to the one my wife and I faced? Do you seek the advice and counsel of someone you trust and respect? Do you seek God's advice?

For Christians, one of the problems frequently encountered is understanding the will of God in a given situation. The late A.W. Tozer believed the choices that Christians must make from day to day fall into one of four categories:

- Those for which God has said an emphatic "No"
- Those for which God has said an emphatic "Yes"
- Those He leaves to your own sanctified preferences
- Those that require special guidance from the Lord[2]

In Jeremiah 29:11, God declares,

"I know the plans that I have for you...."

How do you get in on His plan? How do you determine into which one of these categories your situation fits? Finding God's direction is not as complicated as we often make it seem. There is no mystic puzzle to solve in search of an elusive, hidden truth. No magic formulas, rites, or rituals are required in order to determine God's direction for you. If you eagerly seek it, God will reveal His direction to you. *The Compass* presents some simple principles that can serve as a framework to help you seek, find, and follow God's direction.

In the introduction to the book *Experiencing God*, by Henry Blackaby and Claude King, the authors state,

> Knowing God does not come through a program, a study, or a method. Knowing God comes through a relationship with a Person. This is an intimate love relationship with God. Through this relationship, God reveals Himself, His purposes, and His ways; and He invites you to join Him where He is already at work.[3]

The starting point for this relationship is trusting Jesus Christ as Lord and Savior. Absent from this relationship, you are groping in the darkness and cannot discern God's direction.

> *The man without the Spirit does not accept the things that come from the Spirit of God, for they are foolishness to him, and he cannot understand them, because they are spiritually discerned.*
>
> —1 Corinthians 2:14

If you have not taken this first step of trusting Jesus Christ, the time to do so is now. See *Starting a Relationship with God* (on page 93) for help with this decision. If you have taken this foundational step,

> *This is good, and pleases God our Savior, who wants all men to be saved and come to a knowledge of the truth.*
>
> —1 Timothy 2:3

Whether you are a new or longtime believer, the same question applies: Where do you go from here?

In the story *Alice in Wonderland*, young Alice inquires of the Cheshire cat:

> *"Would you tell me, please, which way I ought to walk from here?"*
> *"That depends a good deal on where you want to get to," said the cat.*
> *"I don't care much where," said Alice.*
> *"Then it doesn't matter which way you walk," said the cat.*[4]

Regarding the direction for your life, do you care where you go, or are you, like Alice, indifferent?

What do you want to accomplish during this study? For what specific decision(s) in your life would you like to know God's direction? What are the questions for which you seek answers?

Consider these questions; then, in the space below, write down the situations and decisions for which you will specifically seek God's guidance during this study.

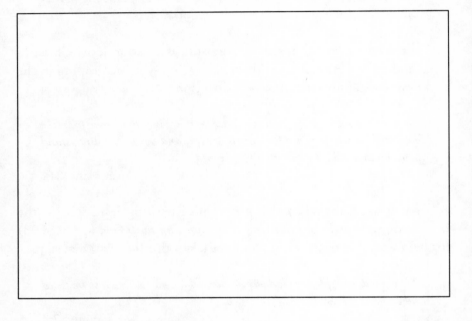

Over the next twenty-eight days, you will study simple, yet life-changing truths and promises from Scripture to help you seek, find, and follow God's direction. It is my prayer that through this study you will (1) strengthen your relationship with God, (2) grow in faith, and (3) respond in obedient action...

So that the body of Christ may be built up, until we all reach unity in the faith and in the knowledge of the Son of God and become mature, attaining to the whole measure of the fullness of Christ.
—Ephesians 4:12-13

Week One

Renewing Your Mind

*Do not conform any longer to the pattern of this world, but be trans-
formed by the renewing of your mind. Then you will be able to test and
approve what God's will is—his good, pleasing and perfect will.*
                                                                —Romans 12:2

Is that all there is to it? All you have to do in order to determine
God's will and direction is to renew your mind! But how do you accomplish this? How do you renew your mind? I would like to know
because there are times when I think I have lost mine!

The devotions this week focus on some practical steps to assist you
with this transforming renewal of your mind.

Day 1: Surrender Your Will

"...If anyone would come after me, he must deny himself and take up his cross and follow me."

—Matthew 16:24

Have you ever participated in a political poll? It is intriguing and frustrating how the pollsters phrase the questions and choices of answers in order to elicit the response they want.

Yet, how many times, when faced with a crisis or critical decision, do you approach God in the same manner? You have a direction or list of options all worked out and you want God to affirm and bless your plans or pick from your list of acceptable options. Can you think of a time in your life when you approached God in this manner? Describe that time in the space below.

A first step in renewing your mind is surrendering your preconceived ideas, your will, and opening your heart to God so that He can influence your thinking.

You were taught, with regard to your old self, which is being corrupted by its deceitful desires; to be made new in the attitude of your minds; and to put on the new self, created to be like God in true righteousness and holiness.

—Ephesians 4:22-24

Surrendering your will does not mean that you do not have any choices or are not allowed to make any decisions in life. On the contrary, God created you with an intellect and free will, and He expects you to use them for His glory.

> *And whatever you do, whether in word or deed, do it all in the name of the Lord Jesus, giving thanks to God the Father through him.*
>
> —Colossians 3:17

Under the umbrella of your love for Him, your love for others, and consistency with the guidance and instruction of the Scriptures, God may leave many, if not most, decisions in life to your personal preferences.

> *Delight yourself in the* LORD *and he will give you the desires of your heart.*
>
> —Psalm 37:4

However, God may at any time intervene and provide specific instruction for a circumstance or decision in your life. Therefore, it is vitally important that you surrender your will so that you are prepared to hear from God.

George Müller was an evangelist and philanthropist in England in the 1800s. He was also a man of great faith whose life demonstrated the power of prayer. He wrote the following about ascertaining the will of God:

> I seek at the beginning to get my heart into such a state that it has no will of its own in regard to a given matter. Nine-tenths of the trouble with people is just here. Nine-tenths of the difficulties are overcome when our hearts are ready to do the Lord's will, whatever it may be. When one is truly in this state, it is usually but a little way to the knowledge of what His will is.[1]

A good point of beginning for you may be the prayer of David in Psalm 139:23:

Search me, O God, and know my heart; test me and know my anxious thoughts....

Make this your prayer and ask God to show you the mindset (your will) that you need to surrender so that He can reveal His will to you. List the things you need to surrender in the space provided below.

Day 2: Be Still

"Be still, and know that I am God...."

—Psalm 46:10

We live in a hurried world. Demands for your time bombard you from all sides. Do you use a daily planner or personal organizer? Even if you do not, you are probably familiar with these organizational tools. The following table represents a schedule from a daily planner. For each hour, fill in the activities for a "typical" day in your life.

6:00 A.M.		3:00 P.M.	
7:00 A.M.		4:00 P.M.	
8:00 A.M.		5:00 P.M.	
9:00 A.M.		6:00 P.M.	
10:00 A.M.		7:00 P.M.	
11:00 A.M.		8:00 P.M.	
Noon		9:00 P.M.	
1:00 P.M.		10:00 P.M.	
2:00 P.M.		11:00 P.M.	

Busy—for many of you this word may best describe your days, each crammed full with activities. Your time is becoming the most precious commodity of your life. You know that building relationships takes time as well—time spent together, talking together, getting to know each other better. Think about the closest relationships in your life. Is time together necessary in developing and maintaining these relationships? Or perhaps better questions might be these: Where do you invest your time? Is this where you find your closest relationships?

You cannot manage time. There are twenty-four hours in every day; however, you can manage yourself within the time that you have. How much time do you spend driving each day? When you get into your car, do you, like me, out of habit immediately turn on a CD or the radio? Do you turn on the TV whenever you are home, even if you are not watching it?

As noted in the introduction, knowing God comes through a personal relationship with Him. How much time during each day do you devote to building your relationship with God? We could all invest more time in our relationship with God. Even in your prayer times you can shut God out by rattling off your prayer list and adding, "in Jesus name, *amen!*" If you are to know God, to know His direction, you must practice the discipline to still your lips, your heart, and your mind, and simply listen.

One day as I reached to turn on my car radio, I felt the nudge of the Holy Spirit saying, *"Don't touch that dial! Tune in to me instead."* Now I steal away at least a few minutes of silence each day as I drive, listening to what God has to say.

Oswald Chambers, in his devotional classic *My Utmost for His Highest*, expressed this truth well:

> Get into the habit of saying "Speak, Lord," and life will become a romance (1 Samuel 3:9). Every time circumstances press in on you, say, "Speak, Lord," and make time to listen.[2]

In the space below, list some specific ideas that you can use each day in order to "be still" and listen.

Write a prayer of commitment to God that incorporates at least one of these ideas to which you commit in order to make time each day to "be still" and listen to Him.

Day 3: Saturate Your Life with God's Word

Fix these words of mine in your hearts and minds; tie them as symbols on your hands and bind them to your foreheads. Teach them to your children, talking about them when you sit at home and when you walk along the road, when you lie down and when you get up. Write them on the doorframes of your houses and on your gates, so that your days and the days of your children may be many in the land that the LORD swore to give to your forefathers....

—Deuteronomy 11:18-21

The imagery in these verses is vivid and very tangible. So much so that observant Jews interpreted these verses literally, writing the law on strips of parchment and placing them in two small leather boxes called phylacteries, one strapped to the forehead and one around the left arm. But what is God communicating to us in these verses?

Fix these words of mine in your hearts....–They are to be the very core of your being: shaping your thoughts, igniting your passions, showing your errors, and equipping your spirit to fulfill God's purposes (see 2 Timothy 3:16-17).

...and minds; tie them as symbols on your hands and bind them to your foreheads....–You are to commit them to your memory, so they are always at the forefront of your thoughts. His words are to guide and be evidenced by the work of your hands.

Teach them to your children....–You are to *teach* them to your children, not just expose your children to them (e.g., take them to church and hope it soaks in somewhere along the way). You are to instruct, explain, and ensure understanding.

...talking about them when you sit at home and when you walk along the road, when you lie down and when you get up.–You are to make them prominent in your home and present in your travels. From your first waking moment until you lie down to sleep, they are to permeate your life: any time, any place, all the time, every place.

Write them on the doorframes of your houses and on your gates....–You are reminded to take them with you as you leave your home, no matter where you go. And when you return, you are reminded to take them inside with you again. They are to be the banner over the gates of your life, posted for all who enter in or pass by to see.

   ...*so that your days and the days of your children may be many in the land that the LORD swore to give to your forefathers....*–They are a conduit of God's blessing in your life. They are inherently life transforming.

> *As the rain and the snow come down from heaven, and do not return to it without watering the earth and making it bud and flourish, so that it yields seed for the sower and bread for the eater, so is my word that goes out from my mouth: It will not return to me empty, but will accomplish what I desire and achieve the purpose for which I sent it.*
> —Isaiah 55:10-12

If you think of your life as a sponge and God's Word as water, are you dry and shriveled; saturated and overflowing; or somewhere in between? What actions will you take in order to saturate your life with God's Word? Prayerfully consider the measures you will take and write your plan of action below:

Some ideas to consider:
    Start a daily devotional time
    Participate in a weekly Bible study
    Memorize Scripture
    Listen to the Bible on CD

Let the word of Christ dwell in you richly...
—Colossians 3:16

Day 4: Do Not Worry

"Therefore, I tell you, do not worry about your life, what you will eat or drink, or about your body, what you will wear. Is not life more important than food, and the body more important than clothes?"

—Matthew 6:25

worry (wûr´ē) v. 1. to feel uneasy or concerned about something; be troubled. Synonyms: brood, dwell, fret, mope, stew; these verbs mean to turn over in the mind moodily and at length.

Worry is the antithesis of a positive mental outlook. Romans 8:28 says,

And we know that in all things God works for the good of those who love him, who have been called according to his purpose.

The foundation of worry is a lack of faith and trust in the sovereignty of God and in the truth of His Word. Worry ought to be for you a flashing alarm, reminding you to examine your thoughts and refocus on God. Worry accomplishes nothing and, even more importantly, a consequence of worry and negative thinking is that you may completely miss God's direction. Perhaps there is no greater example in Scripture of the consequences of worry than the account of the Israelites in Deuteronomy 1:19-36:

- God told the Israelites to take possession of the land He had given them.
- God said, "Do not be afraid; do not be discouraged."
- They sent spies to scout out the land.
- The spies returned with the fruit of the land saying, "It is a good land the LORD our God is giving us."
- However, the spies also reported that the people there were powerful, living in fortified cities (see Numbers 13:27-28).

On what part of the report did the people focus? They fixated on the negative.

> *But you were unwilling to go up; you rebelled against the command of the LORD your God. You grumbled in your tents....*
> —Deuteronomy 1:26-27

They lacked faith in the sovereignty of God and in the truth of His Word. They focused on the problems and ignored God's promise. God said that He had already given them the land, and so there was, in reality, no problem at all. All they had to do was trust and obey, but they didn't. As a result,

> *When the LORD heard what you said, he was angry and solemnly swore: "Not a man of this evil generation shall see the good land I swore to give your forefathers, except Caleb...."*
> —Deuteronomy 1:34-36

When you focus on the negative, when you worry, you will not experience:

- **God's Peace**—*That night all the people of the community raised their voices and wept aloud. All the Israelites grumbled....*
  —Numbers 14:1-2

- **God's Blessing**—*"...They will meet their end in this desert; here they will die."*
  —Numbers 14:35

- **God's Presence**—*"Do not go up, because the LORD is not with you."*
  —Numbers 14:41-42

About what circumstances in your life do you feel worried or anxious today? Write a prayer and talk to God about them as you would to your best friend.

Cast all your anxiety on him because he cares for you.

—1 Peter 5:7

Day 5: Focus on the Positive

...whatever is true, whatever is noble, whatever is right, whatever is pure, whatever is lovely, whatever is admirable–if anything is excellent or praiseworthy–think about such things.

—Philippians 4:8

As my older brother drove home from college one weekend, the fan belt on his old jalopy broke, leaving him stranded on the side of the interstate a few miles from home. A passerby gave him a lift into town. My father was home recovering from heart surgery, and my mother needed to remain at home to care for him. So off my brother and I went, first to the auto parts store and then back to his car on the side of the interstate.

Amazingly, we attempted to replace the fan belt in spite of our utter ignorance of auto mechanics. In mid-repair, we realized that his blinking hazard lights had run the battery down and the car would not start. No problem! I would simply turn my car around on the shoulder so we could jump start his. Being a relatively new driver, I maneuvered cautiously in order to avoid the cars speeding by on the interstate, so cautiously that my rear wheels dropped off the shoulder and began to spin on the wet, sloping ground. Now I was stuck, my car perpendicular to my brother's car and the interstate, but not close enough for the jumper cables to reach.

My brother walked to the nearest exit, found a service station, and called home. My mother loaded Dad into their car and began driving to pick up my brother while I, for some reason that must have seemed logical at the time, waited on the side of the interstate, guarding two incapacitated vehicles.

As my mother, who was a little preoccupied, approached the dimly lit service station to collect my brother, she cut the corner into the drive a little too closely, and both of the front wheels dropped off into a ditch. Now they were stuck, and she felt afraid that she had killed my dad (he was fine).

A little while later the station owner and his tractor had my mom and dad's car back on the road, and a tow truck had my car unstuck and was towing my brother's car home (we just thought we had the fan belt on correctly). Somewhere during the return home, my dad remarked to my mother that he sure was thankful. "For what?" she replied. Dad responded, "I am thankful that we only have three cars!"

> *...give thanks in all circumstances, for this is God's will for you in Christ Jesus.*
>
> —1 Thessalonians 5:18

By maintaining a positive attitude and a sense of humor, my father had clearly applied this Scripture to his circumstance.

Romans 12:2 tells us that God's will is good, pleasing, and perfect. You will not find it through cynicism, distrust, doubt, gloom, negativity, pessimism, or skepticism.

Are any of these negative ways of thinking clouding your view today? Is your attitude toward circumstances in your life blinding you to what God wants to accomplish through you? In the space below, write down circumstances in your life for which you need to adjust your perspective and focus on the positive.

Write a prayer of thanksgiving to God regarding these circumstances, confessing your negative thoughts, asking forgiveness, and praising Him for all that He has done and is about to do.

Day 6: Pray Continually

Be joyful always; pray continually; give thanks in all circumstances, for this is God's will for you in Christ Jesus.

—1 Thessalonians 5:16-18

On Day 2 of the study this week you listed the activities for a typical day in your life. Reflect back on this list and answer the following questions:

- With how many people do you communicate during a typical day?
- How many phone calls, e-mails, faxes, cell phone calls, letters (do people still write letters?), and instant messages do you send and receive in a typical day?
- What is the total amount of time that you spend each day communicating with others?

Building and maintaining relationships takes effective and frequent communication. Our relationship with God is no exception.

- What are ways you can use to communicate with God?
- How many times in a week or in a day do you communicate with God?
- How long is the duration between times that you focus on communicating with God?

In the focal Scripture for today, 1 Thessalonians 5:16-18, Paul instructs the members of the church at Thessalonica to "pray continually" and "give thanks in all circumstances." Our lives are to abound with an attitude of gratitude. I was recently reminded that I take much of God's blessing for granted.

As I talked with a friend, who had recently lost his job, about God's provision, he stated that when he took a shower each morning he thanked God for the blessing of hot water. His attitude of gratitude, is spite of his circumstance, challenged me to offer prayers of thanksgiving to God frequently throughout each day.

In the box below, list ways that you can improve your communication with God. The Scripture references may provide some ideas.

Psalm 1:1-2

Psalm 5:3

Psalm 63:6

Psalm 77:12

Psalm 119:97

Mark 1:35

Acts 1:14

1 Thessalonians 5:16-18

Other ideas:

Review your answers to the second three questions on the preceding page. In the space below, write your commitment to improve the quality and quantity of your communication with God. Be specific.

Consider sharing your commitment with an accountability partner.

Day 7: Guard Your Mind

The weapons we fight with are not the weapons of the world. On the contrary, they have divine power to demolish strongholds. We demolish arguments and every pretension that sets itself up against the knowledge of God, and we take captive every thought to make it obedient to Christ.
—2 Corinthians 10:4-5

Satan's objective is your destruction (see John 10:10, 1 Peter 5:8). His target to achieve that objective is your mind.

The battle for the mind began in the Garden of Eden when the serpent asked Eve, "Did God really say...?" She responded by reciting God's command regarding the tree. She clearly knew it. But the serpent persisted, twisting the truth, and planting in Eve's mind a seed of doubt regarding God's command. Her downfall, and ours, is that she entertained and dwelled on thoughts clearly in opposition to God's Word and at some point began to rationalize her disobedience. How often do you and I do the same by conforming our thinking to the pattern of the world, rationalizing our disobedient actions?

Read again the focal verse for this week:

Do not conform any longer to the pattern of this world, but be transformed by the renewing of your mind. Then you will be able to test and approve what God's will is—his good, pleasing and perfect will.
—Romans 12:2

According to this verse, what happens if your thoughts are conformed to the pattern of this world? Write your response in the box below.

How do you overcome this worldly pattern of thinking? You do so by renewing your mind, by:

- Surrendering your will
- Being still
- Saturating your life with God's Word
- Not worrying
- Focusing on the positive
- Praying continually, and lastly,
- Guarding your mind

Have you ever purchased a new vehicle? To what extremes did you go in order to keep it looking new? Did you park at the far end of the Wal-Mart parking lot in order to avoid that first door ding? Surely you should guard your mind with an even greater devotion.

During a time of intense stress in my life, I became discouraged and depressed. I struggled in my own strength, consumed by busyness, doubt, worry, and negative thoughts. I became saturated with cynicism.

In my desperation for God's deliverance, I cried out to Him, and He replied with a passage from the focal verse for today:

...take captive every thought to make it obedient to Christ.

Is this possible? Yes, because with God, all things are possible. How do you take captive every thought? The answer is—one thought at a time. Looking back, I see that I descended to the bottom of the valley one negative thought at a time. The descent took months and it remains a battle that I fight every day.

If you have a computer and Internet access, you are familiar with pop-up advertising—those small, annoying ads that suddenly appear in the middle of your screen. How do you respond to these? You probably click the "close window" button without even reading the ad. Many people install pop-up blocker software to minimize the number of these ads that show up on their computer.

Your mind is the most sophisticated and complex computer ever created. Satan will tempt you with "pop-up" thoughts. You should respond by taking that thought captive to Christ and mentally clicking the ▣ to close the window on that thought. Do not dwell on it or even allow it to remain in the background where you can call it up again later.

You can also minimize Satan's potential influence by guarding the inputs to your mind. Guard what you watch on television, see on your computer, read, hear, etc. These things do affect how you think. If they didn't, advertisers wouldn't spend billions of dollars on them. If you do not guard your thoughts, you give Satan a foothold in your mind that exploits your freedom in Christ. As Paul noted,

> *"Everything is permissible"—but not everything is beneficial. "Everything is permissible"—but not everything is constructive.*
> —1 Corinthians 10:23

What thoughts do you need to take captive today?

Seeking God's Direction

"You will seek me and find me when you seek me with all your heart."
—Jeremiah 29:13

The answers for many questions regarding God's will are already provided in the Scriptures.

Should you forgive someone for what he or she did to you?

...forgive as the Lord forgave you.
—Colossians 3:13

Should you participate in a business venture with high profits, but questionable ethics?

The Lord abhors dishonest scales, but accurate weights are his delight.
—Proverbs 11:1

God's direction for you will never contradict the Scriptures. For circumstances where the correct course of action is not clearly defined by the Scriptures, God desires that we seek His direction.

...First seek the counsel of the LORD.

—1 Kings 22:5

The daily devotions for this week present some tools to help you seek the counsel of the Lord, to seek His direction.

Day 1: Desire God's Direction

In the space below, write in your own words a definition for the word "halfhearted."

What results should you expect from a halfhearted attempt at something? Write your response in the box below.

In Jeremiah 29:13, what is the condition that God gives for finding Him?

Lou Holtz, a legendary college head football coach, built football programs throughout his illustrious career. He is the only coach in NCAA history to lead six different programs to bowl games. He is renowned as a great motivator.

Coach Holtz asked his players three questions:

1. Can I trust you?
2. Are you committed?
3. Do you care?

Coach Holtz knew that halfhearted players could not help a team to accomplish its goals.

How would you rate your desire to seek, find, and follow God's direction? Rank yourself on the scale below by circling the appropriate number (10 is wholehearted, 5 is halfhearted, and 1 is apathetic).

1 2 3 4 5 6 7 8 9 10

Can God trust you to use the time, talents, and resources that He gives you to accomplish His purposes? Can He trust that you will act on His direction when He reveals it?

Are you committed to wholeheartedly following His leadership and direction in your life?

Are you passionate about seeking, finding, and following God's direction? Do you care?

If God were asking you these questions, how would you respond? Write a prayer of reply below.

Day 2: Follow the Direction You've Been Given

... "Well done, good and faithful servant! You have been faithful with a few things; I will put you in charge of many things. Come and share your master's happiness."

—Matthew 25:23

When my son reached driving age, we discussed at length this awesome new privilege. In order for him to acquire the new freedom and new choices associated with driving a vehicle, I had to have confidence that he understood the level of responsibility required and the potential for serious harm to him and others if he did not practice what he learned in driver education, obey traffic laws, and always pay attention. Also, he had to cheerfully use the vehicle to run errands for his parents (yes, even to pick up his sister).

In order to assess his readiness for this new responsibility and his commitment to follow these instructions, I evaluated his obedience in the "little things," the instructions that he already knew regarding the responsibilities that he already had.

Most of us have experienced this principle in our jobs, our homes, volunteer organizations, etc.: demonstrated responsibility in little things leads to greater responsibility. The life of Joseph is an excellent biblical illustration of this principle (see Genesis 39-41). In Matthew 25:23 (shown above) Jesus tells His disciples that this principle applies in the kingdom of heaven as well. Read this verse again.

Write some of the "little things" in which you already know God's direction, along with an assessment of your own obedience in these areas. Some Scripture references are provided to help you get started.

Exodus 20:1-8

Malachi 3:7-10

Matthew 28:19-20

1 Corinthians 13:4-8a

Ephesians 4:32

Philippians 2:14-16

Philippians 4:4-7

Colossians 3:12-17

James 1:19-22

1 Peter 3:7

In his publication *Finding the Elusive Will of God*, Michael Bronson states,

Many Christians make the common mistake of expecting God to provide them more leading and guidance even though they have not been obedient in what God has already shown them. These are often small things such as being truthful with others, treating your mate with respect, obeying the laws of the land, maintaining a pure thought life, etc.[1]

Spend some time in prayer and ask the Spirit to reveal to you areas where you are not following the direction that you have already been given. What actions will you take in response? In the space below, write a prayer of commitment to take these actions.

Day 3: Acknowledge God's Sovereignty

Trust in the Lord with all your heart; and lean not on your own understanding. In all your ways acknowledge him and he shall direct your paths.

—Proverbs 3:5-6 NKJV

The word "sovereign" sounds very important, regal, and authoritative. You may have heard this word in a sermon or a hymn during a worship service. But what do you and I mean when we say that God is sovereign? I like the following definition given in the book *Yet I Will Trust Him* by Peg Rankin.

The sovereignty of God means that God can do anything He wants to do, any time He wants to do it, any way He wants to do it, for any purpose He wants to accomplish.[2]

It is impossible for our finite minds to fully comprehend an infinite God. When I find myself questioning God's ability, trying to convince Him that He must not understand the gravity of a situation, or struggling to believe that He has a situation under control, I turn to Isaiah 40:12 and begin reading:

Who has measured the waters in the hollow of his hand, or with the breadth of his hand marked off the heavens? Who has held the dust of the earth in a basket, or weighed the mountains on the scales and the hills in a balance?

Who has understood the mind of the LORD, or instructed him as counselor? Whom did the LORD consult to enlighten him, and who taught him the right way? Who was it that taught him knowledge or showed him the path of understanding?...

...Do you not know? Have you not heard? Has it not been told you from the beginning? Have you not understood since the earth was founded?

He sits enthroned above the circle of the earth and its people are like grasshoppers. He stretches out the heavens like a canopy, and spreads them out like a tent to live in.

... *"To whom will you compare me? Or who is my equal," says the Holy One. Lift your eyes and look to the heavens: Who created all these? He who brings out the starry host one by one, and calls them each by name. Because of his great power and mighty strength, not one of them is missing.*

Why do you say, O Jacob, and complain, O Israel, "My way is hidden from the LORD; *my cause is disregarded by my God?" Do you not know? Have you not heard? The* LORD *is the everlasting God, the Creator of the ends of the earth. He will not grow tired or weary, and his understanding no one can fathom.*

—Isaiah 40:12-14, 21-22, 25-28

Are there circumstances or problems in your life about which you are anxious, concerned, fearful, frustrated, despairing, confused, discouraged, or hopeless? If so, write them in the space below.

One by one, read each of the items that you listed. After each item, pause and read the following Scripture:

"I am the LORD, *the God of all mankind. Is anything too hard for me?"*

—Jeremiah 32:27

Take a moment to express your faith and write a prayer acknowledging God's sovereignty in these circumstances.

Day 4: Pursue Wisdom

If any of you lacks wisdom, he should ask God, who gives generously to all without finding fault, and it will be given to him.

—James 1:5

Some years ago, my son, only three or four years old at the time, spent a few days with my parents. As my dad and my son sat swinging in the back yard, out of the blue my son asked his grandfather this question:

"Da, do you have wisdom?"

What an unusual and deeply profound question from the mouth of a child. My father does have wisdom, and it is evidenced in his life for all to see. It is a gift so compelling that it was evident even to his precocious, preschool grandson, who, I believe, asked the question as he tried to work out in his forming mind what is so unique about his Da.

In your life experience, whom would you consider to be a person of wisdom? Write his or her name here: _____ .

What characteristics and/or actions of this person lead you to conclude that he or she is a person of wisdom? Write your responses in the area below.

A dictionary definition of wisdom is "the ability to discern what is true, right, or lasting; insight."[3] I have heard it said that true wisdom is the ability to see things through the eyes of God, to view the world from His perspective.

Proverbs 2:1-6 says,

> *My son, if you accept my words and store up my commands within you, turning your ear to wisdom and applying your heart to understanding, and if you call out for insight and cry aloud for understanding, and if you look for it as for silver and search for it as for hidden treasure, then you will understand the fear of the LORD and find the knowledge of God.*

Therefore, the question to you is, "Do you have wisdom?" Are there situations in your life for which you feel that you lack wisdom? If so, list them here.

Are you willing to pursue God's wisdom "as for silver and search for it as for hidden treasure"? Before answering, reflect on the following scriptures:

> *When pride comes, then comes disgrace, but with humility comes wisdom.*
>
> —Proverbs 11:2

> *How can men be wise? The only way to begin is by reverence for God. For growth in wisdom comes from obeying his laws...*
>
> —Psalm 111:10, LB

According to these verses, what interferes with receiving God's wisdom? During a time of prayer and reflection, refer back to your studies from Week 1, asking God if there is anything in your life that is preventing you from receiving His wisdom. If the Spirit brings something to mind, write it below, confess it to God, and then ask God for wisdom; He will give it generously.

Day 5: Humble Yourself

He guides the humble in what is right and teaches them his ways.
—Psalm 25:9

What character traits do you think it takes to be successful in the world today? Write down your thoughts below.

Did humility make your list? Is humility highly valued in our society today? Not very much. As a matter of fact, it seems that the more arrogant and outrageous the behavior, the bigger the celebrity status of a person grows. In contrast, humility is what God desires in our lives.

...And what does the LORD require of you? To act justly, and to love mercy and to walk humbly with your God.
—Micah 6:8

In the previous devotion, you were asked to list the characteristics of a person who possesses wisdom. Did humility make your list? The Scriptures tell that humility is evidence of wisdom.

Who is wise and understanding among you? Let him show it by his good life, by deeds done in the humility that comes from wisdom.
—James 3:13

Humility is a prerequisite to finding God's direction in your life. The absence of humility is pride and arrogance. Pride and arrogance not only blind you to God's direction, but make you subject to the direct and active opposition (discipline) of God.

…God opposes the proud but gives grace to the humble.

—James 4:6

Therefore,

Be completely humble and gentle; be patient, bearing with one another in love. Make every effort to keep the unity of the Spirit through the bond of peace.

—Ephesians 4:2-3

If you truly desire to know His direction, you must walk in humility. Will you humble yourself before Him today by making the following your prayer?

Show me your ways, O LORD, teach me your paths; guide me in your truth and teach me, for you are God my Savior, and my hope is in you all day long.

—Psalm 25:4-5

List below any situations or circumstances in your life where you need to let go of your pride and "walk humbly with your God."

Day 6: Realign Your Priorities

"But seek first his kingdom and his righteousness, and all these things will be given to you as well."

—Matthew 6:33

Caution: Realigning things can be stressful! My wife and I had been married a couple of years, and we lived in a small apartment. The pantry space in the kitchen was particularly small. One day while she was away, I tried to find something in the pantry and concluded that a little rearranging was in order. I was very proud of the new arrangement. She was not!

As I discovered, we had a different set of priorities regarding the organization of the pantry. She had the pantry organized based upon the frequency of use of the items and her ability to see and reach them without a stool. I didn't want my petite wife to drop a can on her head, so I put all the canned goods within easy reach on the bottom shelf, arranged by contents in neat rows. The smaller, lighter and, it turned out, more frequently used items, I placed on the top shelf. (Ladies: Please pause and conclude your snickering before continuing.)

What can you learn from my blunder? One thing to learn, guys, is don't rearrange your wife's stuff (not a particularly spiritual truth, but good to know). Perhaps a broader application is to realize that we all approach life from our own perspectives and biases. When approaching any given situation, we have different priorities upon which we make decisions.

How does this relate to finding God's direction? If you desire to find God's direction, you must realign your priorities with His.

On the left side of the following table, list your life priorities. (Hint: Think about where you spend your time and money. These areas are priorities for you.)

My priorities:	

On the top of the right column write "God's priorities:". Now, prayerfully consider God's priorities for your life, and list them on the right side of the table.

How do these sets of priorities align? If there are areas where they do not align, whose priorities need to change?

"For my thoughts are not your thoughts, neither are your ways my ways," declares the LORD. *"As the heavens are higher than the earth, so are my ways higher than your ways and my thoughts higher than your thoughts."*

—Isaiah 55:8-9

In order to know God's direction, you must realign your priorities with His. Will you?

EPILOGUE:

I now have the joy of watching, with a large grin on my face, my daughter as she occasionally decides to help her mother by reorganizing the kitchen cabinets. That's my girl.

Day 7: Follow Your Leaders

Obey your leaders and submit to their authority. They keep watch over you as men who must give an account. Obey them so that their work will be a joy, not a burden, for that would be of no advantage to you.
—Hebrews 13:17

Throughout all of Scripture, God appointed leaders for His people, from the calling of Abram to Moses, Joshua, and the prophets of the Old Testament. In the New Testament the apostles, Paul, James, and others led the early church and advised the leaders of local churches.

In 1 Peter 5:1-4, Peter wrote,

To the elders among you, I appeal as a fellow elder, a witness of Christ's sufferings and one who also will share in the glory to be revealed: Be shepherds of God's flock that is under your care....

Do you believe that God still appoints leaders (shepherds) for churches today? As you ponder this question, read the verses below from the book of Romans.

Just as each of us has one body with many members, and these members do not all have the same function, so in Christ we who are many form one body, and each member belongs to all the others. We have different gifts according to the grace given us. If a man's gift is prophesying, let him use it in proportion to his faith. If it is serving, let him serve; if it is teaching, let him teach; if it is encouraging, let him encourage; if it is contributing to the needs of others, let him give generously, if it is leadership, let him govern diligently; if it is showing mercy, let him do it cheerfully....
—Romans 12:4-8

In this discussion of the body of Christ (the church), Paul mentions several spiritual gifts. List them below.

What do these verses tell us about leadership? Leadership is a spiritual gift that is given to some for the building up of the church. Read again the New International Version translation of these verses from Romans 12, and circle the words "let him" each time they appear.

- Let him serve
- Let him teach
- Let him encourage
- Let him give
- Let him govern

While the emphasis of these verses is encouragement for you to use your gifts, a dual application is appropriate. You are to use your gifts *and allow others the opportunity to use their gifts*. You need to let God's leaders exercise their gift of leadership.

Read Hebrews 13:17, which is shown at the beginning of today's devotion. What are your responsibilities regarding God's leaders in the church? What does this verse say will happen if you uphold your responsibility?

[empty box]

Will you commit today to use your gifts and to allow others to use their gifts?

Week Three

Finding God's Direction

May the Lord direct your hearts into God's love and Christ's perseverance.
—2 Thessalonians 3:5

The devotions for the first two weeks dealt with renewing your mind and seeking God's direction. Yet, as you actively seek God's direction, this question may remain: How do you know when you have found God's direction? The studies this week provide some general guidelines to help you answer this question.

Day 1: Can You Hear Me Now?

Guard your steps when you go to the house of God. Go near to listen rather than to offer the sacrifice of fools, who do not know that they do wrong. Do not be quick with your mouth, do not be hasty in your heart to utter anything before God. God is in heaven and you are on earth, so let your words be few.

—Ecclesiastes 5:1-2

How did we communicate before cell phones? These days a location where cell-phone reception is poor is a major inconvenience. Have you ever experienced the frustration of a poor cell connection where you can hear the other person, but he or she cannot hear you? A popular commercial for a cell-phone company features a man talking on a cell phone. In order to check the quality of his connection, he pauses every few steps and asks, "Can you hear me now?"

I wonder if God feels this way when He is trying to communicate with us. He can hear us just fine, but all we hear is the static of our busy lives. Sometimes He must bring difficult circumstances into our lives just to get our attention. I can almost hear Him asking, "Can you hear *me*, now?"

When it comes to hearing God's voice, how is your reception? Fill in the signal bars below to rate your reception today:

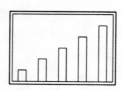

In Mark 4:1-8, Jesus is sitting by a lake and is surrounded by a large crowd. Straining to get near Him, the crowd presses in so closely that He has to get into a boat by the shore. He then teaches the parable of a farmer sowing seeds, in which you find four responses to the hearing of God's Word:

- **The Unprepared Hearer,** whose heart is not ready to receive God's Word, and so Satan is able to quickly take it away (see Mark 4:15). The result is the same as if he or she had never heard God's Word at all.
- **The Superficial Hearer,** who appears to respond but whose desire for God's Word is shallow so that he or she withers quickly when the going gets tough (see Mark 4:16-17).
- **The Preoccupied Hearer,** whose busyness and desire for other things drown out God's Word, so that it produces no fruit in his life (see Mark 4:18-19).
- **The Productive Hearer,** who actively listens, accepts God's Word, and acts on it in faith. This person's life yields a bountiful crop of God's blessing (see Mark 4:20).

Which of the above four kinds of hearers best describes you today?

Jesus concludes the parable of the farmer by saying,

"He who has ears, let him hear."

—Mark 4:9

Can you hear Him now? What will you do to improve your reception?

Day 2: Do You Recognize This Voice?

"My sheep recognize my voice, and I know them, and they follow me."
—John 10:27, LB

From 1952 to 1961 the television show *This is Your Life* was very popular. Each week the show lured to the studio, by some ruse, an unsuspecting person, usually a celebrity. One by one, the host brought out significant people in the guest's life to offer stories from the past. Often, the host introduced a surprise guest from the past with the pronouncement, "Do you recognize this voice?", followed by the guest speaking from off stage.

The question for you today is this: Do you recognize God's voice when He speaks? As you think about this question, take your Bible and read some or all of the following Scriptures. Beside each verse, write the methods through which God spoke.

Genesis 15:1   Matthew 28:5-7
Genesis 28:10-19   John 14:23-26
1 Kings 18:25-39   Acts 4:8-13
1 Kings 19:11-13   Acts 9:4-19
Jeremiah 18:1-10   2 Timothy 3:16

Might God still speak to you in these ways today?

Has God ever spoken to you in one or more of these ways? In the space below, write about that experience.

There is no secret method or formula for recognizing God's voice. It is simply the result of a close, personal relationship with Him. As the examples of Scripture teach us, if you are His and you desire to hear Him, *you will hear and recognize His voice.*

> *He who belongs to God hears what God says. The reason you do not hear is that you do not belong to God.*
> —John 8:47

When He speaks, there will be no doubt about the source or about the direction that He is giving.

> *Whether you turn to the right or to the left, your ears will hear a voice behind you, saying, "This is the way; walk in it."*
> —Isaiah 30:21

The closer your relationship with Him, the more sensitive you are to His voice. Do you have a close, personal relationship with Him? Do you recognize His voice?

Day 3: Are Faith and Action Required?

...faith by itself, if it is not accompanied by action, is dead.
—James 2:17

What is faith? In the space below, write how you would explain to someone else what faith is.

```
┌─────────────────────────────────────────────────────┐
│                                                     │
│                                                     │
│                                                     │
│                                                     │
│                                                     │
└─────────────────────────────────────────────────────┘
```

Do you know someone that you consider to be a person of faith? Write his or her name and why you think of him or her in this way.

```
┌─────────────────────────────────────────────────────┐
│                                                     │
│                                                     │
│                                                     │
│                                                     │
│                                                     │
└─────────────────────────────────────────────────────┘
```

Hebrews 11 is often referred to as the "roll call of faith." Verse 1 of this chapter describes faith as *being sure of what we hope for and certain of what we do not see.* This describes a belief or mindset.

Take your Bible and read Hebrews 11:4-31. In these verses, the writer of Hebrews commends people of great faith. How did the writer know that they had faith? Write your response here.

```
┌─────────────────────────────────────────────────────┐
│                                                     │
│                                                     │
│                                                     │
│                                                     │
└─────────────────────────────────────────────────────┘
```

Did the writer provide a list of the beliefs of these great persons of faith? No, he tells what they did. Actions speak louder than words. We know they believed God by their actions in response to His Word.

Likewise, God's direction for you will require some action on your part. It is not merely an intellectual exercise. God does not call you only to think a certain way or have a certain perspective or system of beliefs. His direction will require action based upon your faith that He will do what He says.

"I am the LORD; that is my name! I will not give my glory to another or my praise to idols. See, the former things have taken place and new things I declare; before they spring into being I announce them to you."
—Isaiah 42:8-9

God will reveal to you what He is doing and what you are supposed to do in response. God never acts in such a way as to make your faith unnecessary. What is God asking you to believe in faith today?

What actions is He asking you to take to demonstrate your faith?

Day 4: Will You Use Your Gifts?

Each one should use whatever gift he has received to serve others, faith-fully administering God's grace in its various forms.

—1 Peter 4:10

When I lived in a different city, the church I attended had a special ministry opportunity each Christmas season. The church had been given a large endowment. Each year, the church used the earnings to purchase clothing and toys as Christmas gifts for needy families in the community.

Volunteers adopted a family, and one Saturday morning in December, a local Kmart opened its doors early just for our church members to take the families shopping. It was a joyous experience, and a humbling one.

Oftentimes, one of the older siblings would ask if he or she could use some of his or her allotted funds to meet a need for some other member of the family. These children who had so little wanted to take their gift and use it for someone else. I will never forget the lesson God taught me through those children.

God has given each of His children gifts, not for our own benefit, but for the benefit of others. These gifts serve two purposes: (1) to build up the church, and (2) to glorify God and point others to Him.

There are different kinds of gifts, but the same Spirit. There are different kinds of service, but the same Lord. There are different kinds of working, but the same God works in all of them in all men. Now to each one the manifestation of the Spirit is given for the common good.

—1 Corinthians 12:4-7

"You are the light of the world. A city on a hill cannot be hidden. Neither do people light a lamp and put it under a bowl. Instead they put it on its stand, and it gives light to everyone in the house. In the same way, let your light shine before men, that they may see your good deeds and praise your Father in heaven."

—Matthew 5:14-16

Do you know your spiritual gifts? If so, write them below.

In the book *The Dynamics of Spiritual Gifts*, William McRae states, "One of the most obvious indicators of God's will for your life is your gift (or gifts)."[1] How are you currently using your spiritual gifts to build up the church, to glorify God, and to lead others to Him? Has God presented you with a new opportunity to use your gifts? If so, describe the opportunity below.

If you have accepted Jesus Christ as Savior and Lord of your life, you have been given spiritual gifts to use for the benefit of others. God will give you opportunity to use those gifts.

If you are unsure of your gifts, contact a church staff member or your Bible study leader. There are some questionnaires that can help you begin the process of discovering your gifts, but the best confirmation is to follow God's direction, accept your assignments, and see your gifts in action.

How will you respond to God's direction to use your gifts?

Day 5: Do You Have God's Peace?

Do not be anxious about anything, but in everything, by prayer and petition, with thanksgiving, present your requests to God. And the peace of God, which transcends all understanding, will guard your hearts and minds in Christ Jesus.

—Philippians 4:6-7

When faced with a significant decision in your life, what emotions might you feel? List some below.

Perhaps you listed things such as excitement, anticipation, apprehension, concern, fear, or uncertainty. How do you work through these emotions in order to reach a decision? List some methods that you have found helpful.

When you follow God's direction, He will give you peace, an internal tranquility that only He can give. This peace transcends all understanding. It is not dependent on circumstances and often exists in spite of them. It is not limited by your abilities, but it is as limitless as

His power that works in you. It is not the result of your reasoning or intellect, but it is the affirmation of His presence within you.

In his book of daily devotions, *My Utmost for His Highest*, Oswald Chambers said it this way:

> God's mark of approval, whenever you obey Him, is peace. He sends an immeasurable, deep peace; not a natural peace, "as the world gives," but the peace of Jesus. Whenever peace does not come, wait until it does, or seek to find out why it is not coming. If you are acting on your own impulse, or out of a sense of the heroic, to be seen by others, the peace of Jesus will not exhibit itself. This shows no unity with God or confidence in Him. The spirit of simplicity, clarity, and unity is born through the Holy Spirit, not through your decisions. God counters our self-willed decisions with an appeal for simplicity and unity.[2]

Are you currently facing a significant decision about an opportunity, situation, or problem in your life? Write the opportunity, situation, or problem in the space below. Then, write the choices or options that you think are available to you.

Pray and ask God for His peace about the direction you should follow. If you do not receive God's peace regarding any of the choices that you listed, He may be telling you to wait, or He may have another direction that you have not considered.

You will keep in perfect peace him whose mind is steadfast, because he trusts in you.

—Isaiah 26:3

Day 6: Stop and Reflect

Since then you have been raised with Christ, set your hearts on things above, where Christ is seated at the right hand of God. Set your minds on things above, not on earthly things.

—Colossians 3:1-2

This week, as you focus on finding His direction, perhaps it is time to stop and reflect.

How do you know when you have found God's direction? As you think about your answer, consider the following questions that summarize the devotions from days one through five of this week.

1. Am I listening for God's voice?
   - Have I prayed about it?
   - Have I surrendered my will?
2. Has God spoken to me about this matter?
   - Through Scripture
   - Through prayer
   - Through circumstances
   - Through another believer
   - Through some other method
3. Are faith and action required?
4. Will I use or discover my spiritual gifts?
5. Do I have God's peace about this matter?

Some of the best advice I ever received was, "When in doubt, don't." If you have God's peace, you will have no doubt about doing something, even though you may have a lot of questions about the details. Following God's direction, even when you don't have all the details, is when faith is exercised and strengthened.

In the company where I work, we use a safety program to encourage all workers to <u>st</u>op <u>a</u>nd <u>r</u>eflect (STAR for short) on the tasks they are about to perform. Each employee is given a small card with a star in the center. The card has key questions to ask before beginning a task. Every employee carries this credit-card sized summary at all times for use as a quick reference. As a result, the safety performance of our facility is the best in our industry and is among the best of all companies operated by our global parent company.

One day, I felt prompted by the Spirit to adapt this concept as a decision-making tool for believers. I hope that you will find it of some use when you are faced with a decision and are seeking God's direction.

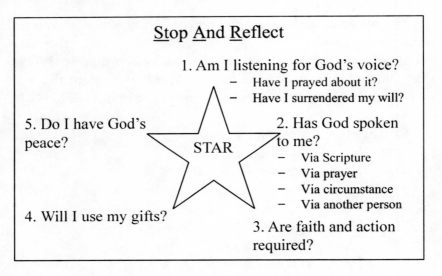

<u>S</u>top <u>A</u>nd <u>R</u>eflect

1. Am I listening for God's voice?
   - Have I prayed about it?
   - Have I surrendered my will?

5. Do I have God's peace?

STAR

2. Has God spoken to me?
   - Via Scripture
   - Via prayer
   - Via circumstance
   - Via another person

4. Will I use my gifts?

3. Are faith and action required?

In his pamphlet *How to Ascertain the Will of God,* George Müller summarized it this way:

> *I do not leave the result to feeling or simple impression. If so, I make myself liable to great delusions.... Thus,*
> *(1) through prayer to God, (2) the study of the Word, and (3) reflection, I come to a deliberate judgment according to the best of my ability and knowledge, and if my mind is thus at peace, and continues so after two or three more petitions, I proceed accordingly.*[3]

Day 7: As Far as You Can Step

I will instruct you and teach you in the way you should go; I will counsel you and watch over you.

—Psalm 32:8

Take a moment and review the previous three weeks of study. In order to seek, find, and follow God's direction you must have a personal relationship with Him through Jesus Christ. Building upon that foundation, you should develop your relationship with Him by:

Renewing your mind:	Seeking God's direction:
• Surrender your will • Be still • Saturate your life with God's Word • Do not worry • Focus on the positive • Pray continually • Guard your mind	• Desire God's direction • Obey the direction that you already have • Acknowledge God's sovereignty • Humble yourself • Realign your priorities • Follow your leaders

You can have assurance that you will find God's direction because you know that:

- He desires a close relationship with you
- He speaks to you
- You will recognize His voice
- He will grow your faith through action
- He will give you the opportunity to use your spiritual gifts
- He will give you His peace when you follow in obedience

Why, then, does finding God's direction seem so difficult? Perhaps it is because we often confuse knowing God's direction with knowing every step, every destination, every stop, every turn, every twist, and every detour along the way.

If you know all these details, no faith is required in order to follow God's direction. Hebrews 11:6 tells us that *"without faith, it is impossible to please God."* The necessity of faith is demonstrated in God's call to Abraham:

> *"Leave your country, your people and your father's household and go to the land that I will show you."*
>
> —Genesis 12:1

He didn't say where the land was or provide instruction on how to get there. In a similar manner, Jesus called Peter and Andrew:

> *"Come, follow me, and I will make you fishers of men."*
>
> —Matthew 4:19

He gave no details, just a call to follow. In each case, God simply required the first step in obedience to the direction given. When you take the first step in obedience, amazing things can happen, as they did when Joshua led the Israelites across the Jordan River into the Promised Land.

> *Now the Jordan is at flood stage all during harvest. Yet as soon as the priests who carried the ark reached the Jordan and their feet touched the water's edge, the water from upstream stopped flowing....all Israel passed by until the whole nation had completed the crossing on dry ground.*
>
> —Joshua 3:15, 17

In her book *As Far As I Can Step*, Virginia Law tells of her missionary days in the Congo. One night a sentry came to her door with a note that another house needed her. It was a very dark, tropical night with no moon or stars shining. The light from the small kerosene lantern in the sentry's hand seemed insignificant against the sea of darkness. "That lamp doesn't give much light, does it?" she questioned. The sentry answered, "No, it doesn't, but it shines as far as I can step."[4]

God will give you light for as far as you can step. Has God shown you a first step that you need to take in obedience to Him? If so, write the step you need to take below.

Will you take this first step?

Following God's Direction

"Whoever serves me must follow me..."

—John 12:26

At the conclusion of yesterday's devotion, you were challenged to take the first step in obedience to direction that God has given you. Will you respond in obedience to God's direction and put your faith into action? This point of decision may be the greatest struggle that you will encounter. Why? Because at this point you must authenticate what you believe, and it is Satan's last opportunity to keep you from taking the first step in obedience to God's direction.

The question for you is the same one that Eve faced: Whom will you believe? Will you believe that God's will for you is good, pleasing, and perfect, or will you believe the lies of the devil? Will you say as Paul said,

...I know whom I have believed and am convinced that he is able to guard what I have entrusted to him....

—2 Timothy 1:12

Day 1: The Decision to Follow

Then Jesus went with his disciples to a place called Gethsemane, and he said to them, "Sit here while I go over there and pray." He took Peter and the two sons of Zebedee along with him, and he began to be sorrowful and troubled. Then he said to them, "My soul is overwhelmed with sorrow to the point of death. Stay here and keep watch with me."

Going a little farther, he fell with his face to the ground and prayed, "My Father, if it is possible, may this cup be taken from me. Yet not as I will, but as you will."

—Matthew 26:36-39

Following God's direction requires a conscious decision to demonstrate your faith by some action. Jesus faced such a decision in the Garden of Gethsemane. He heard the Father's voice and knew the direction He had been given. He had a decision to make, and He understood the cost. Praise God that He obediently went to the cross for you and me!

It always comes down to a decision. Your actions will show what you truly believe and what you don't believe.

Describe a specific circumstance in your life when you had to make a decision to follow God's direction. What decision did you make? What was the outcome?

Are you currently facing a decision concerning God's direction? If so, describe the situation below.

In reality, you face numerous points of decision each day regarding God's will for your life.

- Will you obey the Scriptures?
- Will you honor God?
- Will you forgive?
- Will you act in love?
- Will you respond in anger?
- Will you be truthful?
- Will you gossip?
- Will you give?
- Will you share your faith?

Why not make today your day of decision to follow God's direction?

But if serving the LORD seems undesirable to you, then choose for your-selves this day whom you will serve.... But as for me and my household, we will serve the LORD.

—Joshua 24:14-15

Will you follow Him?

Day 2: The Faith to Follow

One day as Jesus was standing by the Lake of Gennesaret, with the people crowding around him and listening to the word of God, he saw at the water's edge two boats, left there by fishermen, who were washing their nets. He got into one of the boats, the one belonging to Simon, and asked to be put out a little from shore. Then he sat down and taught the people from the boat.

When he had finished speaking he said to Simon, "Put out into deep water, and let down the nets for a catch." Simon answered, "Master, we've worked hard all night and haven't caught anything. But because you say so, I will let down the nets."

When they had done so, they caught such a large number of fish that their nets began to break. So they signaled their partners to come and help them, and they came and filled both boats so full that they began to sink.

When Simon Peter saw this, he fell at Jesus' knees and said, "Go away from me, Lord; I am a sinful man."

—Luke 5:1-8

It had been a long night. The fishermen had plied their trade in the waters of the lake without success in spite of their knowledge, skill, and experience. Tired and disappointed, they began cleaning up their gear to try again another day. Then Jesus entered the picture and instructed them to try again, but this time His way.

I wonder if Simon Peter's voice dripped with sarcasm as he responded to Jesus. I can imagine Peter saying, "Okay, Jesus, we're the professionals here. We've been doing this a long time. We know all about catching fish. Conditions just weren't right last night. Besides, the fish aren't in the deep water this time of year. Nevertheless, because you say so, I will let down the nets. Just don't get your hopes up."

Perhaps this is why, with the boats full of the unbelievable catch, Simon Peter fell at Jesus' knees, declaring, "I am a sinful man."

Do you ever respond to God's direction with skepticism? How often do you, like Simon Peter, think you know more about the situation than God? Do you ever tell God, "That will never work"? Fortunately,

Simon Peter obeyed even if he might have been a tad skeptical. He had enough faith to follow.

Are you presently struggling to find faith to follow God's direction? If so, describe the circumstances below.

In Mark 9:14-27, a desperate father with a demon-possessed son encounters Jesus. As Jesus questions the father about his son's condition, the following conversation occurs:

"It has often thrown him into fire or water to kill him. But if you can do anything, take pity on us and help us."

"If you can?" said Jesus. "Everything is possible for him who believes."

Immediately the boy's father exclaimed, "I do believe; help me overcome my unbelief!"

Do you, just like the boy's father, need to cry out to Him for faith to follow? If so, then pray as the father did, "I do believe; help me overcome my unbelief!" Lord, please give me the faith to follow!

Day 3: The Focus to Follow

Therefore, since we are surrounded by such a great cloud of witnesses, let us throw off everything that hinders and the sin that so easily entangles, and let us run with perseverance the race marked out for us. Let us fix our eyes on Jesus, the author and perfecter of our faith, who for the joy set before him endured the cross, scorning its shame, and sat down at the right hand of the throne of God.

—Hebrews 12:2

Have you ever made a New Year's resolution that you failed to carry out? What was your resolution? What happened? In the space below, write the resolution and why you did not accomplish it.

Perhaps your resolution, like many things in our lives, fell prey to distractions. You lost your focus on the goal. We all have our weaknesses. That container of Turtles 'N Cream ice cream in the freezer often distracts me from my goal of losing some weight! The same can happen regarding God's direction in your life. In order to follow, you must maintain your focus on Him.

What are some things that distract you from following God's direction?

Does the past distract you?

...But one thing I do: Forgetting what is behind and straining toward what is ahead, I press on toward the goal to win the prize for which God has called me heavenward in Christ Jesus.
—Philippians 3:13-14

Do problems or circumstances distract you?

Therefore we do not lose heart. Though outwardly we are wasting away, yet inwardly we are being renewed day by day. For our light and momentary troubles are achieving for us an eternal glory that far outweighs them all. So we fix our eyes not on what is seen, but on what is unseen. For what is seen is temporary, but what is unseen is eternal.
—2 Corinthians 4:16-18

Do selfish desires distract you?

You were taught, with regard to your former way of life, to put off your old self, which is being corrupted by its deceitful desires; to be made new in the attitude of your minds; to put on the new self, created to be like God in true righteousness and holiness.
—Ephesians 4:22-24

Do work, busyness, and "good" activities distract you?

Let your eyes look straight ahead, fix your gaze directly before you. Make level paths for your feet and take only ways that are firm. Do not swerve to the right or the left; keep your foot from evil.
—Proverbs 4:25-27

How do you overcome such distractions and maintain your focus?

Therefore, holy brothers, who share in the heavenly calling, fix your thoughts on Jesus....

—Hebrews 3:1

Where are your thoughts fixed today?

Day 4: The Strength to Follow

For the eyes of the LORD *range throughout the earth to strengthen those whose hearts are fully committed to him....*

—2 Chronicles 16:9

We all have strengths, innate abilities, and talents that God has given us. What do you consider as your strengths?

We also have limitations or weaknesses in our abilities and talents. What do you perceive as your weaknesses? List them below.

Have you ever used your weaknesses as excuses not to follow God's direction in your life? Why? Was it fear of failure? Was it the fear that your weaknesses would be publicly exposed? Describe a time when you used your weaknesses as an excuse not to follow God's direction.

The Scriptures tell us that God is not limited by our weaknesses. As a matter of fact, we are told just the opposite:

"My grace is sufficient for you, for my power is made perfect in weakness."

—2 Corinthians 12:9

How can God work effectively through your weaknesses? Look at your list of weaknesses. How can God perfect His power in you through them? Write your response here.

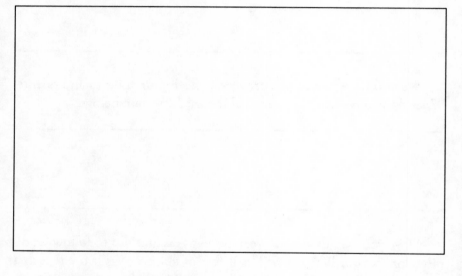

But God chose the foolish things of the world to shame the wise; God chose the weak things of the world to shame the strong. He chose the lowly things of this world and the despised things—and the things that are not—to nullify the things that are, so that no one may boast before him. It is because of him that you are in Christ Jesus, who has become for us wisdom from God—that is, our righteousness, holiness and redemption. Therefore, as it is written: "Let him who boasts boast in the Lord."

—1 Corinthians 1:27-31

God chooses to work through your weaknesses in order that your pride is not a distraction and in order that His power may be revealed.

God will equip you and strengthen you to follow His direction. He gives the promise of His presence and power for whatever He calls you to be, wherever He calls you to go, and whatever He calls you to do. Therefore, instead of giving excuses when you receive His direction, you can declare as did Paul:

I can do everything through him who gives me strength.
                                                    —Philippians 4:13

Let His power give you strength to follow His direction today.

Day 5: The Help to Follow

"But the Counselor, the Holy Spirit, whom the Father will send in my name, will teach you all things and will remind you of everything I have said to you."

—John 14:26

Most likely, all of us, at one time or another, have felt overwhelmed by a task. I feel this way every fall when I look out at the leaves on my yard. They fill hundreds of bags. The thought of tackling this task on my own makes it seem a lost cause. Fortunately, I have help: a riding lawn mower with a bagger—and a teenager! Knowing that I have some help, I feel the task is more manageable.

When God called Moses to lead the Israelites out of Egypt, Moses clearly felt inadequate for the task. In Exodus 3:11 through 4:17, Moses gave God excuse after excuse, but for each of Moses' excuses, God gave the assurance of His presence.

God also gives you help and encouragement to follow His direction. He gives these through:

- The Holy Spirit
- The Scriptures
- Each other

Just as God assured Moses of His presence, He assures His children of His presence through the Holy Spirit.

...the Spirit helps us in our weakness.

—Romans 8:26

Do you feel inadequate for, afraid of, or overwhelmed by a task you must perform in order to follow God's direction?

So we say with confidence, "The Lord is my helper; I will not be afraid. What can man do to me?"

—Hebrews 13:6

Are you discouraged by circumstances? If so, turn to the Scriptures for some encouragement.

For everything that was written in the past was written to teach us, so that through endurance and the encouragement of the Scriptures we might have hope.

—Romans 15:4

The encouragement of the Scriptures is all the more reason to saturate your life with God's Word. As you read of God's unchanging faithfulness, your heart will be encouraged and emboldened to follow His direction.

In addition to the promise of His presence and the encouragement of the Scriptures, He gives us something tangible for today: each other. As the following Scriptures reveal, God does not intend for you to "go it alone" in order to follow His direction.

Carry each other's burdens, and in this way you will fulfill the law of Christ.

—Galatians 6:2

...encourage one another daily, as long as it is called Today, so that none of you may be hardened by sin's deceitfulness.

—Hebrews 3:13

...encourage one another and build one another up....

—1 Thessalonians 5:11

Let us not give up meeting together, as some are in the habit of doing, but let us encourage one another....

—Hebrews 10:25

As you share with other Christians what you believe to be God's direction for you, God will provide an encourager to help you follow His direction. He will also use you to encourage others. Take some time in prayer and ask God to give you the name of a person who needs some encouragement. Write his or her name here _____.
Begin praying now and commit to contact that person within twenty-four hours.

Day 6: The Cost to Follow

"…anyone who does not carry his cross and follow me cannot be my disciple. Suppose one of you wants to build a tower. Will he not first sit down and estimate the cost…?"

—Luke 14:27-28

What does it cost? A reasonable question to ask, and as Jesus states in Luke 14:27-28, it is a question that you should ask. For many, this very question, or the fear of the answer, prevents them from following His direction in their lives.

Matthew 19:16 recounts the story of a rich young man who approaches Jesus, inquiring what he must do to inherit eternal life.

"Why do you ask me about what is good?" Jesus replied, "There is only One who is good. If you want to enter life, obey the commandments."

"Which ones?" the man inquired.

Jesus replied, "Do not murder, do not commit adultery, do not steal, do not give false testimony, honor your father and mother, and love your neighbor as yourself."

"All these I have kept," the young man said. "What do I still lack?"

Jesus answered, "If you want to be perfect, go, sell your possessions and give to the poor, and you will have treasure in heaven. Then come, follow me."

When the young man heard this, he went away sad, because he had great wealth.

Following God's direction will come at a cost. The specific cost in your life is between you and God, literally. As the story of the rich young man illustrates, following God will cost you anything that you desire more than seeking, finding, and following Him.

God wants a relationship with you. So much so that He Himself paid the price in order to make the relationship possible. The price He paid is beautifully expressed in the following lyrics from *Love Song* (words by Johnny Mac Powell, Music by Third Day, CD *Offerings*):

I know that you don't understand the fullness of my love
How I died upon the cross for your sins
And I know that you don't realize how much that I give you
But I promise, I would do it all again

Just to be with you, I've done everything
There's no price I did not pay
Just to be with you, I gave everything
Yes, I gave my life away

What cost are you willing to pay? Will you respond as did the songwriter?

Just to be with you, I'd do anything
There's no price I would not pay
Just to be with you, I'd give anything
I would give my life away.

Therefore, I urge you, brothers, in view of God's mercy to offer your bodies as living sacrifices, holy and pleasing to God....
—Romans 12:1

What will following Him cost you? Write your response below.

Day 7: The Time to Follow

… "I will follow you, Lord; but first let me go back and say good-by to my family." Jesus replied, "No one who puts his hand to the plow and looks back is fit for service in the kingdom of God."

—Luke 9:61-62

Take your Bible and read the following passages of Scripture. As you read, take note of how the people responded when Jesus spoke.

Matthew 4:18-22

Matthew 9:9

Mark 5:35-42

Luke 5:24-25

Luke 19:5-6

John 2:7-9

Even the dead responded immediately! Yet, how many times do we hit the spiritual snooze button and try to put God off?

Satan is a crafty fellow. He knows that it is easier to get you to tell God "Not now" than it is to get you to tell God "No!" Do you tell God that you will get around to that:

- When the kids are grown
- When I get out of debt
- When circumstances are more favorable
- When the risks are less
- When I feel better
- When work slows down a little
- When I have more free time
- When they listen to me

- When they see things my way
- When I see others carrying their fair share of the load
- When I understand
- When I stop hurting

Do any of these sound familiar? What you and I often rationalize as harmless procrastination is, in fact, disobedience. When you tell God "not now," you are really saying, "God, right now there are things I desire more than following you."

Has God given you some direction to which you have been responding "Not now"? If so, write the direction down in the space below.

Read again the focal verses from Luke 9:61-62. When God speaks, the time to follow is *now*. Will you follow His direction now?

Conclusion:
A New Beginning

George Truett, former long-time pastor of First Baptist Church in Dallas, offered this truism: "The greatest knowledge is to know the will of God; the greatest achievement is to do the will of God."[1] The blessing is in the doing!

This author testifies that the blessing is in the doing. The writing of this study has been for me a blessing beyond measure. My profession is chemical engineering, not writing. Some time ago the church my family attends asked me, and I agreed, to serve on a steering committee exploring and executing relocation of the church. As I, in my own heart, began to search out God's will in that process, the Spirit compelled me to write this study. How God will use it, both in and beyond my own life, I do not know. This I do know: God gave me direction, I followed in obedience, the privilege was mine and the glory is His. I present this book back to God as an offering of thanks.

I trust that as you complete this study it is not the end, but a new beginning as you seek, find, and follow God's direction for your life. Go back to the questions that you wrote in the introduction at the beginning of the study. Do you have answers to your questions? Have your questions changed?

I suspect that for many, as for me, the search for God's direction leads me to conclude that I wasn't asking the right questions in the first place. Just like the pollsters, I sometimes start out asking questions, hoping to elicit from God the response I want to hear from my list of acceptable answers. Oftentimes, my questions are not even on the correct topic, my thinking being limited by my will.

Henry Blackaby and Claude King address this issue in the book *Experiencing God*.

> Often people approach knowing and doing God's will this way: They ask, "Lord what do you want me to do? When do you want me to do it? How shall I do it? Where shall I do it? What will the outcome be?"
>
> Isn't this response most typical of us? We are always asking God for a detailed "road map". We say, "Lord, if You could just tell me where I am heading, then I will be able to set my course and go."
>
> He says, "You don't need to. What you need to do is follow Me one day at a time." We need to come to the place where our response to God will be: "Lord, just tell me what to do one step at a time, and I will do it...."
>
> ...When you get to the place where you trust Jesus to guide you one step at a time, you experience a new freedom.[2]

Therefore, if you find yourself back at square one with a new set of questions, don't be dismayed, but instead enjoy your newfound freedom. You do not have to have all the answers. There is no reason to be frustrated if God has yet to reveal His direction. Instead,

> *Keep on asking, and the gift will be given you; keep on seeking, and you will find; keep on knocking, and the door will open to you.*
> —Matthew 7:7, CBW

This verse emphasizes the necessity of persistence and patience in prayer.

God is sovereign and will reveal His direction in the manner and time appropriate to accomplish His purposes. Let us encourage one another as we continue to seek, find, and follow His direction.

Review your notes from each day, and on the following page list any matters that God has placed on your heart during this study. For each item, write the actions that you will take in response. Periodically review, update, and add to this information. Make this list a journal of your faith and God's faithfulness in your life.

I thank my God every time I remember you. In all my prayers for all of you, I always pray with joy because of your partnership in the gospel from the first day until now, being confident of this, that he who began a good work in you will carry it on to completion until the day of Christ Jesus.
—Philippians 1:3-6, CBW

What God placed on my heart:	My action plan in response:

Starting A Relationship With God

The first step in obedience to God is to accept His free gift of salvation through faith in Jesus Christ. The following Scriptures from the book of Romans will guide you with this first step:

- Admit your sin

  This righteousness from God comes through faith in Jesus Christ to all who believe. There is no difference, for all have sinned and fall short of the glory of God, and are justified freely by his grace through the redemption that came by Christ Jesus.

  —Romans 3:22-24

- Accept Christ's sacrifice and God's free gift of eternal life

  But God demonstrates his own love for us in this: While we were still sinners, Christ died for us.

  —Romans 5:8

For the wages of sin is death, but the gift of God is eternal life in Christ Jesus our Lord.

—Romans 6:23

- Confess Jesus as Lord and believe that God raised Him from the dead

    ...if you confess with your mouth, "Jesus is Lord," and believe with your heart that God raised him from the dead, you will be saved.

—Romans 10:9

Please contact your pastor, a church staff member, Bible study leader, or a Christian friend if you have any questions or need help with this decision. If you just made this decision, call someone in the group listed above and share your decision with him or her.

NOTES:

The Compass

Study Guide
for Small Groups

Understanding the Small Group Discussion Guide

Thank you for leading your class or small group through *The Compass,* a four-week series of daily devotions to help people seek, find, and follow God's direction. Designed for the busy times in which we live, each day's devotion is concise, taking only a few minutes to read. However, each day's devotion is intended to stimulate introspection and facilitate spiritual growth on the part of the reader. Each day the reader is asked personal and thought-provoking questions and is challenged to action in response to the truth of God's Word.

The Compass is not a theological treatise on God's will, but utilizes Scripture, quotations, illustrations, and personal stories to provide a framework for the reader to seek, find, and follow God's direction in any situation. *The Compass* is a personal and interactive study, requiring the reader to identify at the beginning of the study specific situations for which he or she seeks God's direction.

Group discussion questions for each week are provided in this study guide. These group questions are open-ended in order to facilitate meaningful discussion. The group questions cover the major concepts from each of the daily devotions for that week. However, the group questions are also intended to be general enough so that even someone who did not have access to or review the studies for the preceding week can participate in the discussion.

The questions from the daily devotions may be too personal for most people to share answers in a group setting. That is Okay; don't press them to do so. As the discussion progresses, some individuals may feel comfortable enough to share personal application or what God revealed to them during the study. The group facilitator can break the ice by being the first to open up and share how God is working in his or her life.

The general and open-ended nature of the group discussion questions may raise as many questions as are answered. Be sensitive to your group members and explore areas where they have questions that are not included in the discussion questions. This is an excellent opportunity to set up an additional discussion time, perhaps in someone's home during the week or over coffee at a restaurant. Promote such opportunities, since they are less formal and provide for more social interaction for people to build relationships.

Here are some suggestions for the small group study:

- Ask one person in each group to be the discussion facilitator.
- For large groups, divide into smaller groups of eight to ten people.
- Give each person a copy of the discussion questions.
- Refer to the daily devotions and Scripture references as you talk about these questions.

Session 1: Renewing Your Mind

SESSION OUTLINE:

Getting to know each other (10 minutes)
Facilitator Overview (5 to 10 minutes)
Discussion Questions (30 to 40 minutes)
Facilitator Wrap-up (if time permits after group discussion) (5 to 10 minutes)

GETTING TO KNOW EACH OTHER:

Have each person give his or her full name and tell something about himself or herself that most people don't know.

FACILITATOR OVERVIEW:

Read Romans 12:2 (NIV) from the introduction to the Week 1 devotions. Where the New International Version says "test and approve," the King James Version says "prove." According to this verse, in order to discern God's will you must renew your mind. Ephesians 4:23 expresses the same truth: *...to be made new in the attitude of your minds; and to put on the new self....* This is a continual process, not an event.

The devotions for Week 1 presented seven practical steps given in the Scriptures to assist you with this transforming renewal of your mind:

- Surrender your will

  – Key verse: *..."If anyone would come after me, he must deny himself and take up his cross and follow me."*
  —Matthew 16:24

- Be still

  – Key verse: *"Be still, and know that I am God...."*
  —Psalm 46:10

- Saturate your life with God's Word

  - Key verse: *Fix these words of mine in your hearts and minds....*
    —Deuteronomy 11:18

- Do not worry

  - Key verse: *"Therefore, I tell you, do not worry about your life, what you will eat or drink, or about your body, what you will wear. Is not life more important than food, and the body more important than clothes?"*
    —Matthew 6:25

- Focus on the positive

  - Key verse: *...whatever is true, whatever is noble, whatever is right, whatever is pure, whatever is lovely, whatever is admirable—if anything is excellent or praiseworthy—think about such things.*
    —Philippians 4:8

- Pray continually

  - Key verse: *Be joyful always; pray continually; give thanks in all circumstances, for this is God's will for you in Christ Jesus.*
    —1 Thessalonians 5:16-18

- Guard your mind

  - Key verse: *...we take captive every thought to make it obedient to Christ.*
    —2 Corinthians 10:5

You will review these again in your group discussion. The first few discussion questions deal with general concepts regarding God's will.

GROUP DISCUSSION QUESTIONS:

1. Read the following statement:
   "For every situation in life there is always a right (or good) choice and a wrong (or bad) choice."
   Do you agree or disagree with this statement? Why?

2. A.W. Tozer said that the choices Christians must make from day to day fall into one of four categories. Discuss some choices you think might fit into each category.
    1. Those for which God has said an emphatic "No"
    2. Those for which God has said an emphatic "Yes"
    3. Those which He leaves to our own sanctified preferences
    4. Those which require special guidance from the Lord

3. What factors or circumstances might determine whether a specific choice falls into Category 4 (requiring special guidance) versus Category 3 (left to our preferences)?

4. Read the following statement:
    "For any situation or decision in life, no matter how small, God may give you specific direction."
    Do you agree or disagree with this statement? Why?

5. List people, groups, and organizations that try to influence your thinking.

    What methods are used to influence your thinking?

6. According to Romans 12:2, what must we do in order to determine God's will?

7. The devotions for each day of Week 1 presented different aspects involved in "renewing your mind," in allowing God to influence your thinking. List these below.

Which of these do you find most difficult? Why?

8. Was there a particular thought or truth from this week's study that really grabbed your attention? If so, please share it with your group.

FACILITATOR WRAP-UP:

Does any group or person have any comments to share?

Are there any questions or areas about which you would like further discussion?

Suggest that the group get together one night this week for more discussion of the devotions from this week, or to discuss the devotions for Week 2.

Close in prayer.

Session 2: Seeking God's Direction

SESSION OUTLINE:

Getting to know each other (10 minutes)
Facilitator Overview (5 to 10 minutes)
Discussion Questions (30 to 40 minutes)
Facilitator Wrap-up (if time permits after group discussion) (5 to 10 minutes)

GETTING TO KNOW EACH OTHER:

Have each person give his or her full name and tell where he or she was born and raised.

FACILITATOR OVERVIEW:

Ask: "Does anyone have any additional thoughts to share from Week 1: Renewing Your Mind"?

The devotions this week focused on seeking God's direction. This statement seems obvious, but the first step is that we must have the desire to know His direction.

Jeremiah 29:13 says, *"You will seek me and find me when you seek me with all your heart."*

In your group discussions, you will explore the conditional promise of this verse, along with the following actions that you need to take in the process of seeking His direction.

- Follow the direction you've been given

  - Key verse: ... *"Well done, good and faithful servant! You have been faithful with a few things; I will put you in charge of many things. Come and share your master's happiness."*
    —Matthew 25:23

- Acknowledge God's sovereignty

  - Key verse: *Trust in the Lord with all your heart; and lean not on your own understanding. In all your ways acknowledge him, and he shall direct your paths.*
    —Proverbs 3:5-6 NKJV

- Pursue wisdom

  - Key verse: *If any of you lacks wisdom, he should ask God, who gives generously to all without finding fault, and it will be given to him.*
    —James 1:5

- Humble yourself

  - Key verse: *He guides the humble in what is right and teaches them his ways.*
    —Psalm 25:9

- Realign your priorities

  - Key verse: *"But seek first his kingdom and his righteousness, and all these things will be given to you as well."*
    —Matthew 6:33

- Follow your leaders

  - Key verse: *Obey your leaders and submit to their authority. They keep watch over you as men who must give an account. Obey them so that their work will be a joy, not a burden, for that would be of no advantage to you.*
    —Hebrews 13:17

DISCUSSION QUESTIONS:

1. Read Jeremiah 29:13. What is the condition that God gives for finding Him when we seek Him?

2. In your own words, write what you think the phrase "with all your heart" means? What attitudes and actions would someone who is seeking God with all his or her heart demonstrate?

3. Read Revelation 3:14-16. What do you think Jesus meant by each of the following terms:

Hot –

Lukewarm –

Cold –

In your opinion, why would Jesus rebuke "lukewarm" people, saying He preferred that they were "cold"?

Do you think Revelation 3:16 has application with regard to seeking God's will? If so, what application can you make?

4. List some things that can keep you from discerning God's will.

5. List words or phrases that you think describe God's sovereignty.

6. Do you think that pursuit of "good" things can prevent us from receiving God's "best," His will, for our lives? Give some examples.

7. List the titles for each day's devotion from Week 2.

   Which of these do you think are the greatest struggles for most people? Why?

FACILITATOR WRAP-UP:

Does any group or person have any comments to share?

Are there any questions or areas about which you would like further discussion?

Suggest that the group get together one night this week for more discussion of the devotions from this week, or to discuss the devotions for Week 3.

Close in prayer.

Session 3: Finding God's Direction

SESSION OUTLINE:

Getting to know each other (10 minutes)
Facilitator Overview (5 to 10 minutes)
Discussion Questions (30 to 40 minutes)
Facilitator Wrap-up (if time permits after group discussion) (5 to 10 minutes)

GETTING TO KNOW EACH OTHER:

Have each person give his or her full name, favorite movie of all time, and why it is his or her favorite.

FACILITATOR OVERVIEW:

Ask: "Does anyone have any additional thoughts to share from Week 2: Seeking God's Direction"?

The studies for Week 3 dealt with finding God's direction. Assuming that you are renewing your mind by:

- Surrendering your will
- Being still (listening)
- Saturating your life with God's Word
- Focusing on the positive
- Avoiding worry
- Praying continually
- Guarding your mind

and that you are actively seeking His direction by:

- Following the direction you've been given
- Acknowledging God's sovereignty
- Pursuing wisdom
- Humbling yourself
- Realigning your priorities
- Following your leaders

the question remains: How do you know when you have found God's direction?

In the devotions for Week 3, the study gave five questions to answer in order to help you know when you have found God's direction:

1. Am I listening for God's voice?
2. Has God spoken to me?
3. Are faith and action required?
4. Will I use my spiritual gifts?
5. Do I have God's peace?

You will explore these in more detail in your group discussion.

DISCUSSION QUESTIONS:

1. Review the four responses, or types of "hearers," that Jesus describes in Mark 4:1-8. For each of the four categories, write the description (attitudes, actions, etc.) of a hypothetical person who might represent that type of hearer.

2. What are some things that can prevent us from hearing and/or recognizing God's voice?

3. What are some ways that God speaks? List some different methods, past and present. Do you think God speaks differently today than He did 2,000 years ago?

4. What role do you think spiritual gifts play in helping you to find God's direction?

5. How would you describe God's peace? What does it feel like to you?

6. "A journey of a thousand miles must begin with a single step."

—Lao Tzu, 6th century proverb[1]

Discuss how you can apply this non-biblical proverb to the matter of finding God's direction.

7. What are five questions that you can ask yourself to help find God's direction?

How do your answers to these questions help you to decide whether or not you have found God's direction?

FACILITATOR WRAP-UP:

Does any group or person have any comments to share?

Are there any questions or areas about which you would like further discussion?

Suggest that the group get together one night this week for more discussion of the devotions from this week, or to discuss the devotions for Week 4.

Close in prayer.

Session 4: Following God's Direction

SESSION OUTLINE:

Getting to know each other (10 minutes)
Facilitator Overview (5 to 10 minutes)
Discussion Questions (30 to 40 minutes)
Facilitator Wrap-up (if time permits after group discussion) (5 to 10 minutes)

GETTING TO KNOW EACH OTHER:

Have each person give his or her full name and favorite hobby or recreational activity.

FACILITATOR OVERVIEW:

Ask: "Does anyone have any additional thoughts to share from Week 3: Finding God's Direction"?

In your study during Week 3, you learned five questions to ask yourself to help you discern God's will:

1. Am I listening for God's voice?
2. Has God spoken to me about it?
3. Are faith and action required?
4. Will I use my spiritual gifts?
5. Do I have God's peace?

If you know God's direction, you have reached a point of decision: Do you follow or not? Henry Blackaby calls this the "crisis of belief."[2] Will you take God at His word or not? You must make a decision. However, as the studies from Week 4 show, you are not alone. God will give you:

- The faith to follow

  - *Key verse: …"I do believe; help me overcome my unbelief!"*
  —Mark 9:24

- The focus to follow

  - *Key verse: Let us fix our eyes on Jesus, the author and perfecter of our faith, who for the joy set before him endured the cross, scorning its shame, and sat down at the right hand of the throne of God.*

    —Hebrews 12:2

- The strength to follow

  - *Key verse: For the eyes of the LORD range throughout the earth to strengthen those whose hearts are fully committed to him....*

    —2 Chronicles 16:9

- The help to follow

  - *Key verse: "But the Counselor, the Holy Spirit, whom the Father will send in my name, will teach you all things and will remind you of everything I have said to you."*

    —John 14:26

As you will explore in your group discussions, there is a time and a cost to following God's direction.

DISCUSSION QUESTIONS:

1. Is faith necessary for each of the following activities? If so, in whom or what do you place your faith?
   - Choosing a career
   - Getting married
   - Buying a car
   - Flying on an airplane
   - Having surgery

2. Discuss whether you agree or disagree with the following statements and why:
   "Everyone places faith in something daily; the question is in whom or what?"

"Faith is the absence of doubt."

3. How is faith proven?

    In Mark 9:14-27, how did the boy's father prove his faith?

4. What things might inhibit or distract us from acting in faith?

5. Read Luke 14:27-28 and Matthew 6:24. What do you think these verses tell us about the cost of following God's direction?

6. Is there a cost for following God's direction? If so, what is it?

7. Discuss the following statement:
    "Delayed obedience is disobedience."
    Do you agree or disagree with this statement? Why?

FACILITATOR WRAP-UP:

Recap the conclusion. Ask the class to look back at the questions they wrote down in the introduction to the study. Did anyone's questions change? If so, how? Did anyone receive an answer he or she would like to share?

Does any group or person have any comments to share?

Suggest that the group continue to meet at least monthly in order to encourage each other to seek, find, and follow God's direction.

Close in prayer.

Endnotes

INTRODUCTION

[1] Berra, Yogi, and Dave Kaplan, *When You Come to a Fork in the Road, Take It,* (New York: Hyperion, 2001).

[2] Tozer, Aiden W., qtd. in "Guidance: Knowing God's Will." *Now,* May 1975. Ed. Richard LeTourneau.

[3] Blackaby, Henry T., and Claude V. King, *Experiencing God*, (Nashville: Broadman and Holman Publishers, 1994), 1.

[4] Carroll, Lewis, *Alice in Wonderland,* in *England in Literature,* Eds. James E. Miller, Jr., Myrtle J. James, and Helen McDonnell. (Glenview, IL: Scott Foresman and Company, 1976), 459.

WEEK ONE: RENEWING YOUR MIND

[1] Müller, George, *How to Ascertain the Will of God*, (Bristol, England: ECL).

WEEK TWO: SEEKING GOD'S DIRECTION

[1] Bronson, Michael, "Finding the Elusive Will of God", in *Finding the Elusive Will of God,* 18. http://www.biblehelp.org/will.htm.

[2] Rankin, Peg, *Yet I Will Trust Him*, (Ventura: Regal Books, 1988), 25.

[3] *The American Heritage Dictionary of the English Language*, 4th ed. (Boston: Houghton Mifflin Company, 2000), 1974.

WEEK THREE: FINDING GOD'S DIRECTION

[1] McRae, William J., *The Dynamics of Spiritual Gifts*, (Grand Rapids, MI: Zondervan, 1976), 35.

[2] Chambers, Oswald, *My Utmost for His Highest: An Updated Edition in Today's Language,* Ed. James Reimann, (Grand Rapids, MI: Discovery House Publishers, 1992), December 14.

[3] Müller, George, *How to Ascertain the Will of God*, (Bristol, England: ECL).

[4] Law, Virginia, *As Far As I Can Step*, (Waco, TX: Word Books, 1970), 157.

CONCLUSION

[1] Truett, George W., qtd. in "Toolkit," *Cell Church*, Winter,1996,10. http://www.bible.org/illus.asp?topic_id=1685

[2] Blackaby, Henry T., and Claude V. King, *Experiencing God*, (Nashville: Broadman and Holman Publishers, 1994), 21.

SMALL GROUP DISCUSSION GUIDE

[1] Chan, Wing-tsit, *The Way of Lao Tzu*, in *Bartlett's Familiar Quotations* by John Bartlett (Boston:Little, Brown, & Co., 1968), 74b.

[2] Blackaby, Henry T., and Claude V. King, *Experiencing God*, (Nashville: Broadman and Holman Publishers, 1994), 133.

Printed in the United States
127846LV00005B/22-45/A

9 781414 107547